JOURNEY TO HIGH OFFICE

The Political Campaign

Nancy Lazarus

What this book is about

This book highlights the important issues the general public expects of those aspiring to win legislative seats.

1.CAMPAIGNING FOR YOUR SEAT

A legislator is expected to be informed of the pressing needs of the electorate. This involves going out to the public to interact with the electorate. What do people want? What do you hope to do differently from what is currently happening? Be pragmatic. Do not bring your far fetched dreams into your election campaign.

- Use your strengths. While you campaign under the banner of your party's name, you are the individual who will represent the wishes of people in your constituency and will work with the general public to realize their needs.
- Don't campaign using the true or false faults of the opposition. People want to know what you as an aspiring legislator can offer.
- Avoid personal attacks of other contenders, their background, families or otherwise. This does not address the needs of the electorate.

- Refrain from inciting people to be lawless and destructive. It is retrogressive to destroy what is in place. Seek ways to improve what is in place.

- Avoid sowing seeds of hatred and division among people who may have different thoughts and opinions from yours. As a legislator you stand for and promote peace, law and order.

- Do not be tempted to buy votes. Don't dish out perishable handouts or money to prospective voters. People want lasting life changing developments that transform their lives. If people think you have something to offer they will vote for you.

- The electorate can be persuaded to be on your side. They should not be bullied or coerced and threatened into voting for you. Don't harm political opponents through physical harm, character assassination or property destruction etc. These are criminal acts and not politics.

Relationship with the electorate

- Go to the electorate and persuade them to give you their time.

- Do not abuse the electorate.

- You must draw a line between matters of national interest and personal interest. Work with the young people to improve their plight and groom them for future leadership and to become objective members of society with aspirations to improve themselves and the society at large.

2. METHODS OF CAMPAIGNING

There are several ways to talk to the electorate. You need to think of how to be heard by the housewife, the busy shop keeper, the millenniums voting for the first time, the busy traveler etc.

- **Dialogue**: Talk to people face to face using the individual approach and persuade them to be on your side. Those who have different opinions from yours are not enemies; they could one day vote for you if your party brings about positive changes for example.
- **Use small group approaches** in villages, pubs, clubs and workplaces.
- **Use Written messages**: Send letters of invitation to your speech days; put up posters, drop off flyers, in places frequently visited by people such as restaurants, trains, buses advertise yourself and your planned meetings in newspapers and explain who you are and what you are offering.

- **Use Social media:** Send e-mails, use Twitter, Facebook, Instagram, whatssap and target the people likely to use this type of media
- **Large group methods.** If you must use rallies:
- Inform people about the dates of your rallies but, **Never** force people to attend your rallies.
- Remember that rallies are impersonal. Rallies talk down on people, people want opportunities to express their needs and ask questions.
- Arrive at meetings on time. Don't expect the electorate to leave their work and wait for you. It is rude and disrespectful. Adults value their time and have work to do in their homes, fields and work places.
- Use simple language when talking to the electorate. Some of the people may be illiterate. Leave complex language for when you discuss with your fellow legislators or with journalists.

- Discuss important issues. Avoid wasting people's time. People have other responsibilities they can use their time for.

- Prepare a speech and when you have delivered it leave and let people get on with their lives.

- The electorate does not owe you anything. You are the one who needs their vote. Don't demand anything from the electorate and don't expect and accept gifts from them.

- Don't intimidate people and threaten them with reprisals (e.g. We will take the land away from you, we will not develop this area if you don't vote for me, we will close the country borders). You should persuade the electorate to like you and convince them that you can bring about meaningful changes to their way of life and that you can put forward their needs to government.

3. WHAT DOES THE ELECTORATE EXPECT OF THEIR MP?

- You will represent the electorate and ensure that their needs are heard by government. You will participate in crucial debate in the formulation of policy. You are expected to critically look at the flaws of the current laws and suggest better alternatives. These tasks demand that one is able to understand and translate policy, represent the electorate and work with communities to achieve policy objectives.

- You have got to be of sound education to understand policy, developmental issues, technology, innovation, equity and to articulate the electorate's needs.

- Your charisma, power, riches and who you know do not matter because there is work to be done in specific ways.

- If you don't have the right credentials you pull the country down because you take long to understand issues under discussion, you cannot articulate the policy and may have problems in expressing yourself clearly.

Why do you want the legislative seat?

- You want to participate in creation of laws that govern the country.
- You want to critically debate proposed laws before they are passed into laws
- You want to participate in crucial debate that amends laws.
- The seat enables you to represent the wishes of the constituency.
- Always put the wishes of the people first.
- You are not elected to become a formidable heckler of other legislators presenting the needs of their constituencies
- You don't get a seat to sleep during debates; you are expected to make active constructive national contribution.
- Parliament is not a forum to settle personal scores. Remember you are elected to perform

a national duty and are paid using the taxpayer's hard earned money.

4.WHAT DO YOU TALK ABOUT SHOULD YOU BE ELECTED TO HIGH OFFICE?

- Understand the topic under discussion in order to make meaningful contributions.
- Contribute intelligent well constructed and orderly facts.
- Make useful informed argument about national issues under discussion.
- Talk about policy not about your personal disputes and grudges with an individual person.
- Argue about issues of national interest not personal issues.
- Prepare informed notes that you can take back to the electorate.

Format of your speech:

- **Introduction** (State what you intend to discuss in brief), I would like to address the following: 1.Land 2. Technology 3. Transport in my constituency.

- **Body of your speech** (say what you want to say about the above)
- **Summarize your points**, State how this contributes to solving national problems or how it retards constituency and national development or how it impacts on the welfare of people or disadvantaged groups.

Understand the policy

- Read the policy document over and over to understand it. This makes you able to give your electorate correct information. If you don't understand any aspect of the policy, ask the informed fellow politicians, informed society, lawyers, and university lecturers. You are surrounded by informed people; tap on their knowledge.
- Stick to the policy during your discussions. Don't add your wishes.
- Refer to policy all the time.

Being on the opposition bench

- Participate in debates or issues under discussion.
- Propose new laws based on facts.
- Propose amendments of current laws if you understand them and the impact they may have on the general public.
- Have your points that support your proposal written clearly and put them across clearly without unnecessary emotion.
- Listen carefully to debates and oppose policy not individuals.
- Don't personalize national issues.
- Don't use abusive language. Have your facts written down.
- Don't oppose for the sake of opposing. Have your supporting facts written out clearly.
- Don't disrupt and interject others. They too must have an opportunity to air their views.
- Wait for your turn to speak.
- Exercise tolerance. Not every legislator is likely to present issues you like to hear.

5.BEING A MEMBER OF THE RULING PARTY

- The ruling party does not know everything that a country needs. Not every legislator may agree with your proposals.

- Be objective and tolerant when the opposition present their sentiments. You need to hear those diverse thoughts to improve and strengthen policies.

- A legislative house without opposition is blind and on a train to doom.

- Welcome and listen to criticisms and suggestions from the opposition; through them you correct mistakes, refine laws and redirect efforts towards national objectives.

- Put the country first in all your proposals.

- Don't personalize comments and suggestions

- Don't impose your will even if you are on the majority side.

- Don't threaten the opposition they are only reminding you to take the will of the rest of the country at heart and that your point is not acceptable to all.

- Intelligent people deliver their informed speeches and give others opportunity to air their views.

- Remember that at the end of the day, a country's successes are rated on the total GDP and not the number of successful members of the ruling party.

- Don't impose your will in the constituency. You are not the boss. Remember you also have members of the opposition in the same constituency. You are not necessarily the cleverest person by virtue of aspiring for the legislative seat; there are many educated people in the constituency. Consult them.

6.KNOW YOUR CONSTITUENCY

- Visit your constituency and have set dates, places and times when you can hold consultations with your constituency.

Example:

Every 1st Tuesday of the month Mr. Zero will be at Zizi Hall from 1000hrs to 1400hrs.

Every 2nd Tuesday Mr. Zero will be at Dove Elementary School Hall from 8am till1200hrs

Every 3rd Tuesday Mr. Zero will be at Zai College Hall from 1100hrs to 1500hrs

Every 4th Tuesday Mr. Zero will be at Zenga Pub hall from 1400hrs till late.

- Make the timetable available everywhere in your constituency so that people know when you are visiting their area and they can bring their requests to you.

- Be where you should be promptly. Don't keep people waiting.
- Give each person waiting time to express their pressing need.
- Listen, Talk and Ask. Take notes and find solutions to people's problems
- Let the electorate know you and you them.

Working with People

- Don't take advantage of the people-don't force people to agree with you
- Don't abuse people by taking away their rights (water, electricity, health, food) and freedoms (speech and expression,)
- Don't abuse national resources to gag people
- Don't use the political platform to settle personal scores
- Avoid love for cameras and playing to the gallery at rallies.
- Do not abuse public funds, property, services for personal gains. Don't dip your fingers into

national coffers. A country's resources belong to all of the people, supporters of the ruling party, the opposition and the neutral.

Know each group, who is who?

What are the group concerns of widows, youths, married, teachers, nurses, economists, pensioners etc.? What are their needs? Unite the groups don't divide them.

Identify needs

Who says there is a need?

- Listen, listen, listen, to the electorate. They know what they want.
- Do not impose your ideas and wishes on the electorate

What kind of a need is it?

- Let the constituency describe the nature of their need.

Is it a felt need?

- How many people think it is a need? You must always go with the majority needs

Is it a comparative need?

- Is your electorate comparing events in other constituencies? Study what is happening in other constituencies and provide the electorate with correct information.
- Do not push your electorate to adopt ideas. Give them time to think about new ideas. They may have their own pressing needs.
- Work with your electorate to prioritize their suggestions
- Welcome suggestions and ideas from your constituency. There are plenty of learned people in your constituency. Befriend them and tap on their knowledge and ideas.

7.WHO CALLS THE SHOTS?

- You are **not** the boss. You are a servant of the people. Listen to what people want.
- Don't take unilateral decisions.
- Consult with the constituency.
- Involve the electorate all the way. Let them make the decisions and plans.
- Identify resources that are required to accomplish or fulfill the need.
- Study the feasibility of the project.
- Consult with relevant authorities to see if the idea can materialize.
- Come back to your constituency with feedback

Where should you make a difference?

- Use funds equitably. Don't make meaningful development in your own area or village only. The electorate hates selfish legislators.
- Develop the community not individuals
- Services should benefit all

- Remember you are there to promote development not to retard it. Do not use public funds for your own personal needs. You must be accountable for all the money meant for the public.

Don't make promises.

- Listen to the constituency
- Consult with sources of resources before responding

Objectivity

- Your constituency will have people of diverse thoughts. Tolerance is the key. Different opinions make a debate fertile and help you to see an idea from different angles.
- Decipher sense, truth, and genuineness, relevance of information you hear or that is given to you.
- Think straight. Don't sing praises for your party when things are going astray.

What the electorate expects

- Always be smart, trustworthy and keep out of shady deals
- Avoid scandals (money laundering, embezzlement and other monetary abuses).
- Be exemplary. Avoid womanizing.
- If you have skeletons behind your cupboards, resign and give way to people with a clean track record.

Waning Support

You should know that people no longer want you if

- The numbers of your followers decrease.
- You hear discerning voices in the communities and the media.
- You have nothing more to offer.
- Fresh minds and thoughts are emerging; make way for them. Don't fight them.

8.PRESIDENTIAL ASPIRATION?

So you are aspiring for a presidential post?

In addition to the parliamentary/congressional issues above, you now have to think outside your small constituency.

You now have to think of the country's issues and make them your responsibilities.

This is a mammoth task that you cannot manage single handedly.

Being head of the country may not necessarily mean that you are the best person in the country. It is the same as an open competition for a single vacant or advertised post. Sometimes people get posts because they had courage to go for the post. People get posts because they seemed genuine and informed but put in positions they may not be aware of the detailed knowledge of requirements of the post.

- You need to be an honest person. You need to have trustworthiness. You need to love your country as a whole and its contents, people and natural resources.

- You cannot afford to single out certain groups or ignore certain groups. The whole nation matters and looks up to you for their needs.

- You need to be surrounded by informed people who will bring to the table informed ideas, suggestions and problem solving skills that help you in planning and decision making. You need these knowledgeable people to plan strategies give you answers to impromptu questions and to give you content of your speeches.

Discuss issues with your advisors before you address the public or meetings.

You cannot afford to forget what you said the previous day. There has to be a record of your speeches and you can refer to them. The media will quote and record your words and use them to discredit you.

- You need to carry yourself well everyday and wherever you are.

- You need to be a good public speaker with experience of parliamentary procedures. You will be the most important person in parliament as every the whole legislative team looks up to you for wise leadership.

- Have your facts handy. Have your advisory team close by. People don't want their time wasted with empty promises and unfocussed waffling.

- Every member of society looks up to you for wise leadership. People always have their expectations about the leader. People hope that their problems will be solved, difficult issues in their lives resolved and that you will move them towards prosperity.

Some things people are interested in can be summarized into the following questions:

What will you do for me?

People choose new leaders not just for change of face but because they have personal needs and aspirations they want to accomplish.

Using Maslow's hierarchy of human needs, every individual is aspiring to get essential basic needs in life. People need lower levels needs such as food and shelter and seek opportunities and an ideal climate to improve and progress to the next level.

- How will your leadership satisfy or meet people's aspirations and individual needs? These are the facts that the electorate want to hear in your campaigns.

9.WHAT WILL YOU DO FOR THE COUNTRY?

The societal groups such as women, children, youth, professionals, farmers, the elderly, the disabled, to name but a few, all wait to hear what you can offer them.

What are your visions?

Be informed of what is happening on the ground now in order to take the country forward. How will you make things better?

You must have a domestic policy that addresses people's needs and concerns in the state.

As a prospective country leader, you cannot have expertise in all fields.

- You should plan and identify informed people who become teams of experts, advisors and planners in every sector. Experts must be chosen according to their capabilities and not because they are your friends or you grew up together.

- Maintenance, preservation and upgrading of what is in place as well as creating new ventures increases employment, improves the product and encourages innovation.
- Inform the electorate how you plan to lead people towards achievement of this goal.

Your plans must clearly inform the electorate how you intend to manage resources equitably and distribute them equally to the population.

Food

- A healthy nation is well fed. Hungry people are disgruntled and have little contribution to the development of the country.
- Your internal or domestic policy should spell out how domestic policy will ensure that every mouth is fed and that essential resources will be made available to ensure that the country has adequate food. What will your agricultural policy bring to the farmer and the population?

Do farmers currently have access to adequate land, inputs like fertilizers, draft power, seed, irrigation facilities, food processing industries and means for agricultural research and tapping into export market? What are the prices of basic commodities? Can the ordinary person survive? How will your policies plan to improve the current situation?

Can the farmer continue to produce food items given the cost of production and the prices for goods your government offers?

Will your policies ensure adequate food production and prevent famine for your people and importation of basics?

Housing

A roof over one's head is one of the basic human needs. Poor housing is associated with poverty and disease especially communicable diseases. Prevention of communicable disease is a marker of a nation's state of health. Every person needs decent housing. What will the prospective head of state have in his policy about addressing housing issues in his domestic policy?

Safety

Establishment and maintenance of the rule of law ensures that people are safe they can walk freely and go about their business without fear. What policy does the prospective head of state have in place to ensure that people are served by trained police and other safety personnel like the army, the air force and auxiliaries? These are some of the safety issues people may want to hear in the campaign speech of the prospective head of state.

Health

Good national health includes establishment of new facilities as well as development of existing facilities for the nation. Training and retention of health personnel ensures that the health of the nation is maintained and is progressive. Without good health, the country cannot progress. It is important that an aspiring head of state has a health plan that addresses people' health needs and how the to maintain and improve people's health especially issues about access to essential health care services when one needs them.

Education

The prospective or aspiring head of state must have in place a sound education policy. Education drives development. Without good education there is no development. The education policy must address all age groups to include pre-school, the school age child, the adolescent, young adult and the mature people. There have to be relevant programmes, institutions and personnel to design, implement and maintain as well as improve relevant age specific education for the nation.

The prospective head of state must inform the electorate of plans to establish good national education system.

The Economy

What are the new inventions and technology or additions your government can bring to the economy? This involves enabling and empowering scientists to do their job with ease and without impediments.

How will the new president create jobs, prevent unemployment and make goods available for the domestic market?

Will there be plans to produce excess products for the local markets as well as foreign markets? The electorate want to hear such developmental plans and the pros and cons of adopting such plans.

10.FOREIGN POLICY

A prospective head of state knows what is happening in other countries and makes plans to establish ties with as many other countries a possible.

It is important to establish relations in the region and internationally.

The electorate is interested in knowing how the state contributes to the world peace and the country's preparedness for promoting peace regionally and locally and how these events impact on your country's policies.

Use diplomacy in commenting about events in other countries to maintain good relations with other countries. Good international relations are to the advantage of every country as cooperation that can improve the country can be realized.

Foreign Trade

The electorate wants to know the trade plans of the prospective leader and prospective employment creation through trade.

The electorate wants to hear investment plans and

creation of employment and development.

You want to cut the cost of production.

What is cheaper for your country to acquisition of raw materials and complete products and informing the public about the advantages and disadvantages of both in view of employment creation and decreasing unemployment?

Learn from the mistakes made by other leaders, present or in history and avoid taking previously perilous paths for your country.

Consult, consult, and consult with people.

Do not assume that your individual thoughts represent the minds of the electorate. You are only but just a chairman of the many advisory committees, boards, meetings and groups that inform you of people's concerns, needs, fears and expectations. It is a position that requires social skills of continuous communication and interaction in order to serve all people.

Do no make the mistake of threatening people with reprisals because they have the power to decide if you will hold office or not.

Make your speeches factual, don't just waffle. It pays to have your speech neatly written and follow each point. Many aspiring leaders fall by the wayside by trying to speak off the cuff. You have to have public speaking skills and a focused mind if you take that route. You are likely to stumble and discredit yourself.

Your promises must have a foundation that makes sense to the electorate. Do not just blurt out promises from the top of your head without feasible plans to make them into reality. Don't hope to earn votes through bribing people by promising them the moon before proving that you can provide basics.

People come to your meetings with varying agendas. Do not assess your popularity by the size of crowds that attend your meetings or the number of flashing cameras around you. The crowds that follow you can make or break you in your pursuit of the highest office.

- Some come to take pictures when you make the worst gestures.
- Some come to pick the most foolish statements you make.
- The majority come to assess and analyze the presidential or ministerial substance in you; your tone of voice, your choice of words, diplomacy, your knowledge of current issues, knowledge of history and foreign relations, your sentiments and level of concern about current problems in the state, your problem solving ideas, your respect for the public.

People are not looking for charisma in a leader, or the amount of money, cows, cars, women/men you have had or businesses you have. People are searching for effective leadership skills in the prospective leader. People are looking for a leader who is a peacemaker, someone who cares about them and their welfare as a people; someone who does not take them backwards but propels the country forward.

You win people's support not by fighting your personal wars in public through back stabbing other contenders but by proving to people that you know what the office you aspire for is about and you can manage to hold the country in one piece moving it forward.

Know when to quit

Should you be elected to the high office, listen to the voices around you. The high office is not a right; it is a privilege. Objective leaders take turns to rule.

Why should you go for a second term if you are not managing? Must you stay there until people throw shoes and egg at your face? Must you stay there until the walls around you are falling? Once you start grooming your wife and toddlers for the office then you should know that you have over-stayed your welcome to the State residency and high office.

Must you stay put until you don't remember the day of the week? Only dictators go for the third and umpteenth term of the head of state. If you care to think of the reasons you must stay in office, in most cases they come back to you. It means you have become egocentric. You no longer have the people or country at heart. If records were to be read, you probably have something to hide. In short you have become a dictator. Leave office when you have run out of ideas and leave fresh minds to lead.

www.ingramcontent.com/pod-product-compliance
Lightning Source LLC
Chambersburg PA
CBHW060343290526
45791CB00004B/1517